This book is for

_____

With love

_____

On this date

_____

ZONDERKIDZ

I Can Read My Illustrated Bible
Copyright © 2020 by Zondervan
Illustrations © 2020 by Peter Francis

An **I Can Read Book**

Published in Grand Rapids, Michigan, by Zonderkidz. Zonderkidz is a registered trademark of The Zondervan Corporation, L.L.C., a wholly owned subsidiary of HarperCollins Christian Publishing, Inc.

Requests for information should be addressed to customercare@harpercollins.com.

Library of Congress Cataloging-in-Publication Data

Francis, Peter, illustrator.
     I can read my illustrated Bible : for beginning readers /
     illustrated by Peter Francis.
Description: Grand Rapids, Michigan : Zonderkidz, 2020.
Identifiers: LCCN 2019044566 (print) | LCCN 2019044567 (ebook) | ISBN
  9780310766797 | ISBN 9780310766728 (epub)
Subjects: LCSH: Bible stories, English.
Classification: LCC BS551.3 .I24 2020 (print) | LCC BS551.3 (ebook) | DDC
  220.95/05--dc23
LC record available at https://lccn.loc.gov/2019044566
LC ebook record available at https://lccn.loc.gov/2019044567

Illustrator: Peter Francis
Art Direction & Design: Cindy Davis

Printed in Vietnam

24 25 RRDA 10 9 8 7 6 5 4

Dear Parent:

Your child's love of reading starts here!

Every child learns to read in a different way and at his or her own speed. Some go back and forth between reading levels and read favorite books again and again. Others read through each level in order. You can help your young reader improve and become more confident by encouraging his or her own interests and abilities. From books your child reads with you to the first books he or she reads alone, there are I Can Read Books for every stage of reading:

SHARED READING
Basic language, word repetition, and whimsical illustrations, ideal for sharing with your emergent reader

BEGINNING READING
Short sentences, familiar words, and simple concepts for children eager to read on their own

READING WITH HELP
Engaging stories, longer sentences, and language play for developing readers

READING ALONE
Complex plots, challenging vocabulary, and high-interest topics for the independent reader

I Can Read Books have introduced children to the joy of reading since 1957. Featuring award-winning authors and illustrators and a fabulous cast of beloved characters, I Can Read Books set the standard for beginning readers.

A lifetime of discovery begins with the magical words **"I Can Read!"**

Visit www.icanread.com for information on enriching your child's reading experience.

Visit www.zonderkidz.com/icanread for more faith-based I Can Read! titles from Zonderkidz.

ZONDERkidz

1 BEGINNING READING

I Can Read!

My Illustrated Bible

for **Beginning Readers**

illustrated by
Peter Francis

ZONDER**kidz**

Old Testament

God Made Many Things

Genesis 1–2: Creation

Long ago there was no world.

There was no sun.

There was no moon.

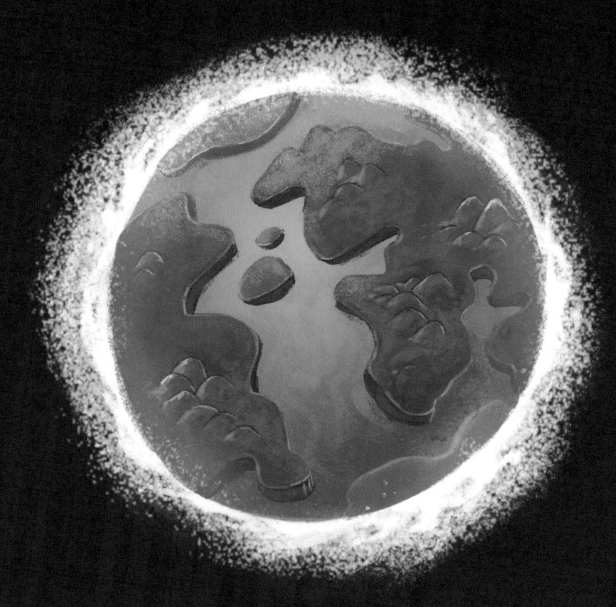

God said, "I will make the world."

So God made the earth.

God said, "I will make the sun and stars."

He said, "They are good."

God made many things.

He made the trees.

He made the fish in the sea.

He made big animals and little animals.

Last of all,

God made a man and a woman.

The man and woman were

happy in God's world.

Something Bad, Something Sad
Genesis 3: Adam and Eve's Temptation

Adam was Eve's husband.

Eve was Adam's wife.

They had a home and food in the garden.

They had many good things.

They were never sad.

But there was one thing
they could not have.
God said, "Do not eat
the fruit on that tree."

16

Adam and Eve did not eat from it.

Then one day a snake talked to Eve.

He said, "This fruit is good.

You should eat some."

Eve knew God would not be happy.

But the fruit looked good.

So Eve ate some.

She gave a piece to Adam.

Adam ate some too.

God was sad they ate the fruit.

Adam and Eve were sad too.

God said, "It is time for you
to leave the garden."

Noah Makes a Big Boat

Genesis 6–7: The Flood and the Ark

Noah was a good man.

He loved God.

One day, God said, "Make a big boat,
Noah. I have a plan."

Noah said, "Yes, I will make it."

God told Noah how to make the boat.

It took a long time.

Then Noah put many animals
and his family on the boat.

One day it began to rain.

It rained and rained.

The water went over the houses.

It went over the trees.

It rained more and more.

The earth was covered in water.

But Noah and his family were safe.

Noah had obeyed God.

God took care of Noah.

Noah said, "Thank you, God."
Noah thanked God for
taking care of him,
his family, and the animals.

A Promise for Abraham

Genesis 18 and 21: A Son for Abraham and Sarah

Abraham and Sarah loved God.

They prayed to God.

They wanted God to be happy.

God loved Abraham and Sarah too.

He gave them many good things.

But there was one thing Abraham
and Sarah did not have.

They did not have a son.

One night, God said to Abraham,

"Try to count the stars."

Abraham saw many stars.

He could not count them all.

God said, "Your family will be like the stars.

I will give you a son.

Your son will have children.

Someday your family

will be too big to count."

Abraham and Sarah had a baby boy.

Abraham said, "God did what he promised.

God gave us this baby boy!"

Abraham and Sarah named their son Isaac.

Jacob Sees a Ladder

Genesis 27–28: Jacob's Dream

Jacob had to leave his home.

He walked miles and miles.

When it was night he
stopped to rest.

That night Jacob had a dream.

He saw a ladder.

It went all the way to heaven.

Angels went up and down the ladder.

Then God talked to Jacob.

"I will go with you," God said.

"I will help you."

Jacob stopped dreaming.

He sat up.

"God was here," he said.

"And God will go with me."

Jacob was happy.

He wanted God to go with him.

He wanted God to help him
on his journey.

God Takes Care of Joseph

Genesis 37–41: Joseph in Egypt

Joseph's father gave him a colorful coat.

This made his brothers mad.

They wanted to hurt Joseph.

One brother said, "Let's kill Joseph."

Another brother said, "No, let's sell him.

He will be a slave and have to work."

So Joseph's brothers sold him.

He went to work in Egypt.

But God took care of Joseph.

Then something bad happened.

A man put Joseph in jail.

God still took care of Joseph.

One night the king had a dream.

He asked, "What does the dream mean?"

No one could tell him.

So a man said, "Joseph can help you."

The man had been in jail with Joseph.

The king called for Joseph.

Joseph told the king what his dream meant.

The king was very happy.

The king said, "Help me take care
of my people."

And God took care of Joseph.

Joseph Forgives His Brothers
Genesis 42–45: Joseph and His Brothers Reunited

Joseph's brothers had been mean to him.

But God took care of Joseph.

He was in charge of the food in Egypt.

One day, Joseph's brothers needed food.

They bought grain in Egypt.

They did not know that the man

who sold them grain was Joseph.

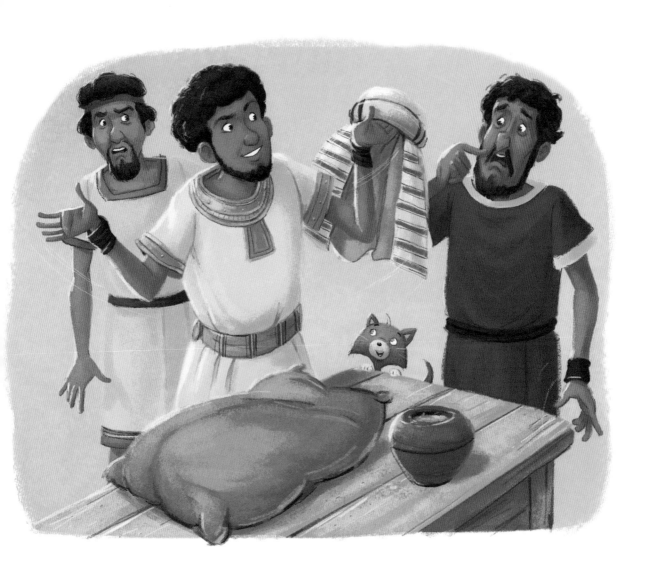

After many days they came back.

They wanted to buy more grain.

Joseph told them who he was.

Joseph's brothers were afraid.

They thought Joseph would kill them.

But he did not!

"I forgive you," said Joseph.

This pleased God.

God wants us to forgive others.

God forgives us too.

Miriam is Brave

Exodus 2: Baby Moses in the Basket

The king did not like God's special people.

He wanted to kill all their baby boys.

Miriam had a baby brother.

Miriam's mom was worried about her baby.

She said, "We must hide your brother."

Miriam's mother made a basket.

She said, "We will put him in this."

She put the basket in the river.

Miriam said, "I will stay with our baby."

She was brave.

Soon a princess came to the river.

She saw the basket and the baby.

She said, "I will keep the baby.

But I will need help."

Miriam ran to the princess.

She said, "I know someone

who will do it.

My mother will take care of him."

Miriam's mother was so happy.

Now her baby would not be hurt.

She said, "Thank you, Miriam,

for being my brave helper."

God Talks to Moses

Exodus 2–4: Moses and the Burning Bush

The baby in the basket was named Moses.

Moses was now a man.

He lived in Egypt.

But the king wanted to kill him,

so he ran away.

Moses was far from home.

His job was to take care of sheep.

Moses looked at his happy sheep.

He said, "My people back home

are not happy. They are slaves."

Moses saw a bush.

It was burning. But it did not burn up!

God talked to Moses from the bush.

God said, "Go back to Egypt.

Get my people away from there."

Moses did not want the job.

He was afraid of the king.

But Moses obeyed God.

Moses went back to Egypt.

He was ready to lead the people.

Going Out of Egypt
Exodus 13–15: The Exodus

God's people left Egypt.

They went as fast as they could go.

Moses led them.

The people knew God was with them.

God was with them in a cloud each day.

Each night the cloud was like fire.

God was showing the people where to go.

One day the people came to a big sea.

They could not go over it.

They could not go around it.

The king and his men were coming.

They wanted to kill God's people.

God made a dry place to walk in the sea.

Moses led the people through the sea.

The king and his men came too.

God made the sea fall on them.

God took care of his people.

He helped Moses lead

them far away from Egypt.

God's Good Rules

Exodus 19–20: The Ten Commandments

The people were near a big mountain.

They heard loud noises.

They were afraid.

But Moses was with them.

God told Moses to go
up the mountain.
Moses obeyed God.
God talked to Moses.

God gave Moses some good rules.

He said, "Tell my people
to obey these rules."

Moses told the people God's rules.

1. LOVE ONLY GOD.
2. GOD IS MORE IMPORTANT THAN THINGS.
3. DO NOT SAY GOD'S NAME IN A BAD WAY.
4. REST ON GOD'S DAY.
5. LOVE AND OBEY YOUR MOM AND DAD.

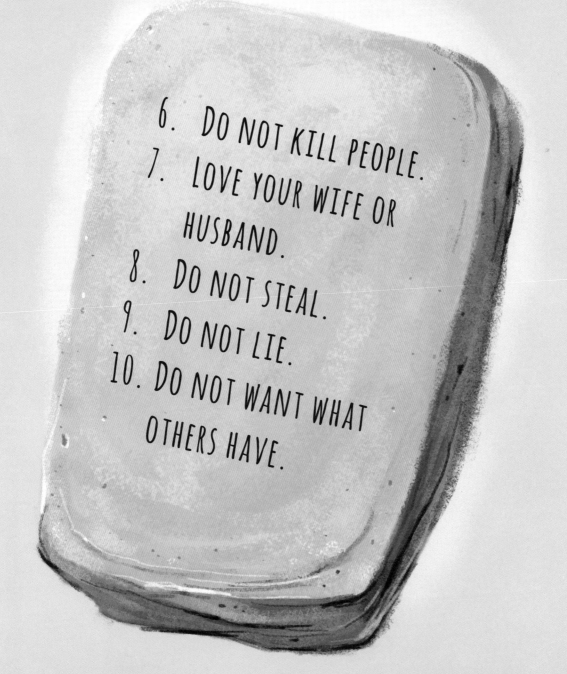

6. Do not kill people.
7. Love your wife or husband.
8. Do not steal.
9. Do not lie.
10. Do not want what others have.

God Helps Joshua

Joshua 6: The Walls of Jericho

God was not pleased with
the people in Jericho.
He told Joshua to fight them.
But God's people didn't know how
to get over the big walls around Jericho.

Joshua said, "God will help us."

God did help Joshua.

He told Joshua how to fight Jericho.

Then Joshua told the people.

Joshua and the people walked
around the walls of Jericho.
Then they went home.
The next day they went
around the walls again.

They did this for six days.

On the seventh day Joshua and the people

walked around the walls seven times.

Then they stopped.

The people of Jericho were afraid.

Joshua and the people began to shout.

The walls of Jericho fell down.

They were able to take the city.

Joshua said, "God helped us do this."

A Man Made Strong by God

Judges 13–16: Samson

Samson was the strongest man of all.

God made him that way.

Samson was a very brave man too.

Some bad people tried to kill Samson.

They did not like Samson's people.

But Samson was too strong for them.

Then Samson told the people a secret.

"If you cut my hair, I won't be strong."

That did not please God.

God said, "Now Samson will not be strong."

The bad people took Samson away.

The people made Samson work for them.

They made him go to their temple.

The people made fun of Samson.

Samson was sad that he had not pleased God.

Samson prayed to God.

He asked God to make him strong again.

God did.

So Samson knocked down the temple.

A Boy Gets a New Home

1 Samuel 1–2: Samuel Is Dedicated to God

Hannah wanted a baby so much.

So Hannah asked God for a baby boy.

God did what Hannah asked.

Hannah was so happy with her baby boy.

"I will call him Samuel," she said.

"And I will give him to God."

One day, Hannah took Samuel to
God's house.

Eli took care of God's house.

"Will you help my boy do God's work?"
Hannah asked Eli.

"Yes," said Eli.

Samuel stayed with Eli.

Eli helped Samuel learn about God.

And Samuel helped Eli take care
of God's house.

Hannah came to visit Samuel.

Samuel loved his mother.

He loved Eli too.

And Samuel loved his new home
where he worked for God.

David is Brave

1 Samuel 17: David and Goliath

Goliath was a giant bully.

He said, "Come and fight me."

But God's people would not fight him.

The men were afraid of Goliath.

A shepherd boy named David said,

"I am not afraid. I will fight Goliath."

The king asked, "How?

You are not as big as him."

David said, "God will help me."

So David went to fight Goliath.

He took his sling.

He took five stones.

The big man ran to David.

David talked to God.

He asked God to help.

Then David put a stone in his sling.

Away went the stone.

Down went Goliath.

Goliath had an army with him.

They were afraid and ran away.

The king said, "David is brave!"

God helped David to be brave.

A Wise King

1 Kings 3: Solomon Judges Wisely

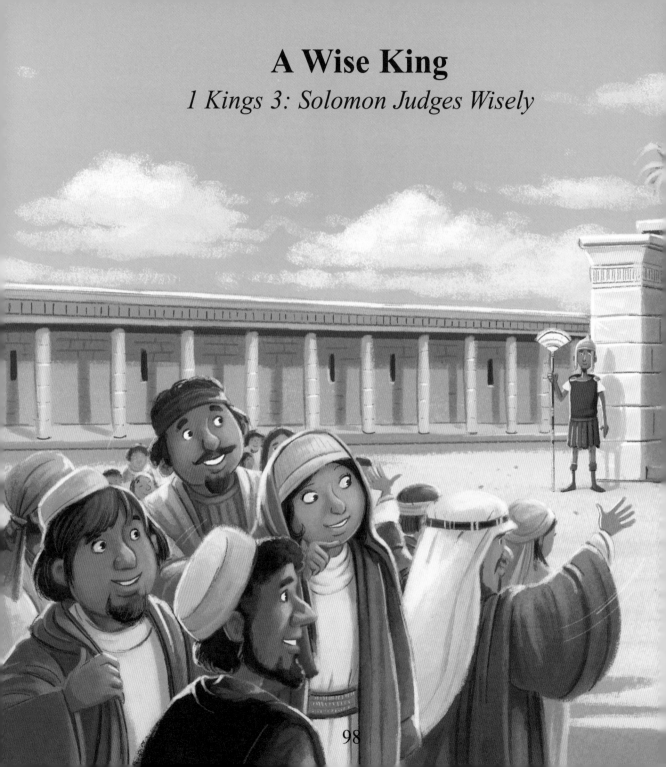

"Long live King Solomon!" the people said.

Solomon was the new king.

He was a very wise king.

He asked God to make him wise.

One day two women came to
Solomon with a baby.
Each woman said,
"This is MY baby."

Solomon did not know who the mother was.

"Cut the baby in two," he said.

"Give some of it to each one."

"NO!" said the mother.

"Yes!" said the other woman.

Then Solomon knew who the mother was.

"Give the baby to the woman who said no," he said.

"Our king is so wise," said the people.

King Solomon said,

"Thank you, God, for showing me

what to do."

Esther Is a Brave Queen
Esther 1–10: Esther Saves Her People

Mordecai came to see Queen Esther.

"Someone wants to kill our people," he said.

"What can I do?" asked Queen Esther.

"Ask the king to help us," said Mordecai.

"The king must ask me to see him.

I could be killed," said Esther.

Esther loved her people.

So she went to see the king.

The king did not kill Esther.

He asked what he could do for her.

"Please help my people," said Esther.

"A bad man wants to kill them.

He will kill me too."

The king did not like this.

He loved Queen Esther.

So the king stopped the bad man.

Now Esther's people were not afraid.

They were happy.

Esther was the brave queen who saved them.

Daniel and the Lions
Daniel 6: God Helps Daniel

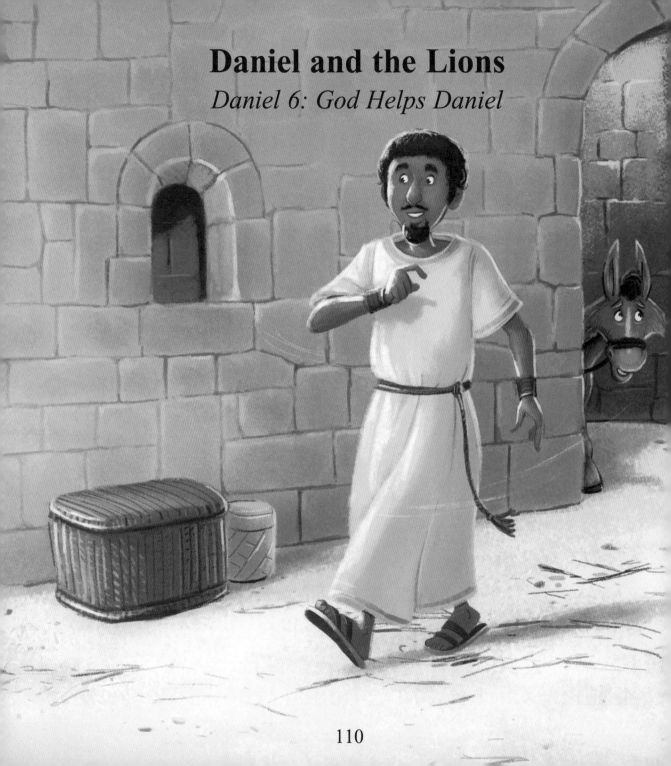

Some leaders were worried

that the king would put Daniel in charge.

They did not like this idea.

They did not like Daniel.

The leaders said, "Make a new rule."

The new rule said no one could pray to God.

If he does, he will be fed to the lions.

The men knew Daniel talked to God.

They knew he would not stop.

Soon they saw Daniel praying to God.

The men ran to tell the king.

The king liked Daniel.

He did not like what these men had done.

But the king had to follow the new rule.

Daniel must be fed to the lions!

The king said, "Your God will help you."

The next day the king went to the lions' den.

Daniel was safe.

The king was happy.

Daniel was happy too.

God had helped him.

Jonah Learns to Obey

Jonah 1–3: Jonah and the Fish

God told Jonah to go to Nineveh.

Jonah did not want to go.

So he ran away on a boat.

Soon a bad storm came!

Jonah said, "I am running away from God.

If you throw me into the water,

God will stop the storm."

The men threw Jonah into the water.

The storm stopped.

Then God sent a big fish.

God told the fish to swallow Jonah.

Jonah was in the fish for three days.

Jonah prayed to God.

He told God he was sorry.

He asked God to forgive him.

God told the fish,

"Let Jonah go."

The fish obeyed God.

It spit Jonah out on land.

Then God told Jonah to go to Nineveh.

This time Jonah obeyed.

He told the people of Nineveh about God.

Jesus Came to Love Us

Luke 2 and Matthew 1: Christ Is Born

Mary and Joseph were going to have a baby.

But they went on a long trip.

Where would they sleep?

The man at the inn said,

"I do not have any room."

The man looked at Mary.

He looked at his animals.

He said, "You may sleep with them.

It is the only place I have."

So Mary and Joseph rested in the barn.

That night Mary had a little baby.

Joseph said, "We will call him Jesus.

God told us to give him this name."

Mary said, "This baby is God's Son.

That is what God told us."

Mary and Joseph said,
"This baby has come to teach
the world about love."

Angels Sing to Shepherds

Luke 2: The Shepherds Visit Baby Jesus

"Look at the sky," a shepherd said.

"It looks like it is day," said another.

"But it is night."

The shepherds were so afraid.

They did not know what the light was.

"Don't be afraid," an angel said.

"I have something to tell you.

There is a new baby in town.

You should go see him.

He is God's Son."

Then more angels came.

They filled the sky.

The angels sang about God.

Then they went away.

"Let's go into town," the shepherds said.

"Let's go see God's Son."

The shepherds ran into town.

They found baby Jesus in a barn.

The shepherds were so happy
to see God's Son!
They wanted to tell others about Jesus.
They told all the people they could find.

The Wise Men Give Their Best

Matthew 2: Gifts for Baby Jesus

A wise man said, "Look! A special star."

Another one said, "I see it too.

We must follow that star.

It will take us to a new king."

The three wise men knew
this new king was special.
He was only a little baby now.
But God had sent him.

The wise men went on camels.

They took their best gifts

to give to the baby king.

They traveled for many days,

following the star.

One day the star stopped.

It stopped over the town of Bethlehem.

The wise men said, "This is the place.

The baby king is here."

The wise men went to see Jesus.

They gave him their best gifts.

They were happy that the star

led them to Jesus.

Jesus is Baptized

Matthew 3: John Baptizes Jesus

Jesus had a cousin.

His name was John.

John lived in the desert.

He ate bugs and honey.

John told the people about Jesus.

He told them to do good things.

He told them to get ready for Jesus.

John told the people how to
make God happy.

Many people listened to John.

They decided to follow God.

John baptized the people in a river.

One day Jesus came to the river.

"I need you to baptize me," Jesus said.

John baptized Jesus in the river.

The Holy Spirit came down from heaven.

The Holy Spirit landed on Jesus.

Then God spoke.

"This is my Son," God said.

"I love him very much."

A Sick Friend

Mark 2: Jesus Heals a Paralytic

Some men asked, "Is Jesus in the house?

Our friend is sick.

Jesus can make him well."

Others said, "Yes, but you cannot get in.

There are too many people."

There were many people in the house.

The men could not get close to Jesus.

They said, "We will go
in another way."

So they put their friend down a hole
in the roof.

They said to Jesus, "Please, help
our friend. He is sick."

Jesus was happy to help their sick friend.

He said, "Get up, you are well."

The man got up.

He was cured.

The man and his friends were happy.

They said, "Thank you! Thank you!"

Jesus Calms a Storm

Luke 8: Jesus Calms the Storm

"Come with me," said Jesus.

"Where?" asked his friends.

"To the other side of the lake," Jesus said.

Jesus and his friends got into their boat.

Soon the boat was out on the water.

Then the wind started to blow.

Faster and faster went the wind.

The boat went up and down on the waves.

Jesus' friends were so afraid.

"Help us!" they said to Jesus.

"The boat is going to sink!"

Jesus looked at the water.

"Stop!" he said.

The wind stopped blowing.

The water was quiet.

The boat stopped going up and down.

"Did you see that?"

one of Jesus' friends asked.

The men looked at Jesus.

"Only God's Son could do that," they said.

A Boy Shares His Lunch

Matthew 14: Jesus Feeds the Five Thousand

"Here is your lunch," a mother said.

"There are five pieces of bread and two fish."

The boy was happy.

He was going to see Jesus.

The boy listened.

Jesus said many good things.

Then Jesus stopped talking.

He could tell the people wanted to eat.

Some men came to the boy.

"May we bring your lunch to Jesus?"

the men asked.

The boy took his lunch to Jesus.

He was happy to give Jesus his food.

Jesus did not eat the lunch.

He broke it into many pieces.

He said thank you to God for food.

He gave the pieces to the people.

Soon all the people had enough to eat.

Jesus smiled at the boy.

"Thank you for your lunch," he said.

The boy smiled too.

Then he sat near Jesus.

The boy ate some bread and fish.

Walking on Water

Mark 6: Jesus Walks on the Sea of Galilee

Jesus said, "It is time for you to go home."

His friends asked, "Will you come with us?"

Jesus replied, "Not right now."

Jesus' friends got into their boat.

They left.

Soon it was night.

The wind began to blow hard.

The water went up and down.

They could not get the boat home.

Suddenly they saw something amazing.
They said, "Look! Who is that
walking on the water?"

The men were afraid.

They said, "It must be a ghost!"

The man on the water said,

"I am not a ghost."

His friends said, "It is Jesus!"

They were happy.

Someone asked, "How can Jesus do this?
Only God's Son can do things like that."

A man said, "Jesus IS God's Son."

Jesus and the Children

Mark 10: Children Come to Christ

Mothers and fathers said, "We want
our children to see Jesus."

Jesus' friends said, "No, not today."

The parents asked, "Why not?"

His friends said, "Jesus is too tired and busy."

Then Jesus walked over to them.

He asked, "What is the matter?"

The parents said, "Your friends will not let our children see you."

Jesus' friends said, "We told them that you
were doing other things."

Jesus said, "Do not tell the children
to stay away from me. They show others
how to come to me."

Then Jesus had the children
come to see him.
He told them many things.
He told them how much
God loves them.

The children asked,

"Do you love us too?"

Jesus said, "Yes, very much.

And I want you to love me too."

Jesus on a Colt

Mark 11: Christ Enters Jerusalem

"I need a little colt," said Jesus.

"It will help me do God's work."

Jesus' friends looked for a colt.

Jesus' friends could not find one.

"Where will we get a colt?" they asked.

Jesus told his friends where to go.

He said a man would give them one.

Jesus' friends went to the man.

"May we give your colt to Jesus?"
they asked.

"Yes," said the man.

He was happy to help Jesus.

Jesus got on the colt.

He went to a big town called Jerusalem.

Many people went with Jesus.

They shouted, "Jesus is our King!"

In Jerusalem Jesus told people about God.

He told them how to please God.

He told them he would die for them.

God had sent Jesus to do these things.

Supper with Jesus

Matthew 26: The Lord's Supper

Jesus and his friends were in Jerusalem.

It was a special time of year.

God's people were celebrating Passover.

It was time to eat dinner together.

Jesus told them, "Eat this bread.

When I am gone do this again and again.

Remember the way I died for you."

Jesus' friends ate the bread.

Jesus said, "Drink from this cup.

When I am gone do this again and again.

Remember the way I died for you."

Jesus' friends drank from the cup.

But his friends were sad.

They did not want Jesus to die.

Suddenly the friends heard

someone singing. It was Jesus.

Jesus' friends began to sing too.

This was an important moment.

Jesus' friends knew he was special.

The Love of Jesus

Matthew 27: The Death of Christ

In Jerusalem, men wanted to hurt Jesus.

One said, "Nail that man
to a cross!"

The men nailed Jesus to the cross.

Jesus had not hurt these men.

But they were hurting him.

Jesus talked to God about these men.

He said, "Forgive them."

The people had not ever seen

a man like Jesus.

They were hurting him.

But he still loved them.

Someone said, "That man is God's Son."

When Jesus died on the cross
he showed the power of love.
He loves us so much that he
died so we can know God.

Jesus Is Alive Again!

John 20: Mary Sees the Risen Christ

Jesus' friend Mary was so sad.

Jesus had been killed.

She went to see where they put him.

But Jesus was not in the tomb.

Mary said, "Someone has taken Jesus."

She began to cry.

Then some angels talked to Mary.

They asked, "Why are you crying?"

She said, "Someone has taken Jesus."

Then Mary saw a man coming.

He asked, "Why are you crying, Mary?"

She said, "I cannot find Jesus."

Then the man said, "Mary!"

Mary said, "Jesus! Is it you?"

Now she knew it was Jesus.

Mary was so happy.

She knew that Jesus was God's Son.

Jesus was alive again!

Jesus said, "I cannot stay with you.

I must go back to my home in heaven."

Telling Others about Jesus

Acts 1–8: The Church Grows

Jesus' friends knew he was God's Son.

He had died for them.

Then he came back to live with them
for a little while.

Only God's Son could do that!

Jesus showed people
the way to know God.
He taught them about his love.

Jesus told his friends, "Go to all the world.
Tell people everywhere
about what I did for them."
After Jesus said these things
he went back to heaven.

Soon, Jesus' friends started teaching.

They told people all about Jesus.

They said, "Jesus loves you.

He wants to help you know God."

Many people liked what they heard.

Others said, "Go away."

Even so, Jesus' friends were happy.

Many people loved Jesus.

More Zonderkidz I CAN READ!
books for you to love:

Collect them all!

Visit www.zonderkidz.com/icanread for more faith-based
I CAN READ! titles from Zonderkidz.

More Zonderkidz I CAN READ!
books for you to love:

Collect them all!

Visit www.zonderkidz.com/icanread for more faith-based
I CAN READ! titles from Zonderkidz.

More Zonderkidz I Can Read! books for you to love:

Collect them all!

Visit www.zonderkidz.com/icanread for more faith-based
I CAN READ! titles from Zonderkidz.

 ZONDERkidz
.com